CONFRONTATIONS

with

THE ABSOLUTE

CONFRONTATIONS

with

THE ABSOLUTE

Chaim Kind

Published by Chaim Kind
Henderson, Nevada, 89052

Book Design by Kory Kirby

ISBN 978-1-7346355-0-8

Library of Congress Control Number: 2020902821

Printed in the United States of America

First Edition

www.chaimkind.com

DEFINITION

CONFRONTATION:

An encounter with extremes. A face-to-face reflection. A comparison between ideas that appear/exist in opposition. Opposing forces (parts) that make up the whole.

with:

Association. Connection. Holiness. Separation. Interaction. Communication.

THE ABSOLUTE:

Existence and Emptiness. That which is *beyond* imagination (insight, understanding, and knowledge), and that which is imagination itself. The whole truth as a unified singularity. The all-inclusive mystery of existence. The knowable and the unknowable.

Chaim Kind — 2020

TABLE OF THE ABSOLUTE

(50 poems)

For Sara. This book wouldn't exist without you.
And we made Shua with our love.

CONFRONTATIONS
with
THE ABSOLUTE

THE MYSTIC

Fingers to knuckles to wrists to elbows to shoulders to neck
Through chest to ribs
Through heart to nerves.

Soles to feet to ankles to calves to knees to hips
Through genitals to thighs
Through pelvic bone to spine.

Stomach to lungs to throat to tongue to gums to teeth
Through lips to flesh
Through taste to speech.

Chin to nose to brow to ears to eyes to sight
Through skull to brain
Through water to skin.

Through vacuums to intelligence
Through head to mind
Through neurons to nails
Through hair to imagination
Through space to words
Through blood to veins
Through doorways and windows
Through tunnels and floors.

I surround my arms around my
Body — and touch my
Face — with letters and words:

One question
One answer
One mystery.

THE THINKER

(30 lines)

How to ascend the voice of the thinker?
How to descend reason without the unreasonable?
How to escape language and madness?
And what if madness is playful?
And what if magic is true?

Birthed with hidden thoughts
Polished with fearful thoughts
Broken with truthful thoughts
Molded with honest thoughts.

I philosophized:
Do thoughts think me
Or [...] do I think thoughts?

Escaping systematized thought — is to mistrust thought
Mistrusting my thoughts
Left me trusting mistrust
And seeing both sides of confusion
I saw both sides of clarity
And inside the mirror of endless dialogue.

I fought My self to find my Self
And found The Self in conflict;
Destroying the image I made
Or [...] the image of my image.

I was searching for myself with the image we had made
I was looking for a way through the terror of the grave.

I asked:
Who had the first thought?

Who spoke the first word?
Who formed the first form?

But I couldn't find the end of the circle;
And I couldn't find an uncaused cause.

THE MESSENGER

(12 lines)

The perfect man was murdered by the mind
And I don't mind using his ashes
For the hollow pencil I found.

The perfect woman was hung upside down
And I don't mind using her ink
On the notebook I was given.

When I returned from the cave
    They hit me with sticks
When I returned from the mountain
    They twisted my words
When I returned from the ocean
    They were gone.

THE SHAPESHIFTER

(41 lines)

I move behind the empty space of probability
And guide my voice around the weather.

I fall alongside drawings and arrows
And circle the motions of my compass.

I am being drawn with lead and ink
And pulled by thought and time.

In perception — I belong
With definition — I am gone
There is no pointer and the center — missing.

I will tell you who I am when you are not looking
I will show you the pictures of my dreams.

Between the hemispheres — empty-space
I shift to become both sides of speech.
Between the lungs and the heart
Between the knees and the gut
I become a reaction to my action.

When I greet you in the chamber
Or meet you in the forest;
I will take off my disguise (and my boots)
I will show you the soles of my feet (and my roots)
I will transform my words
But will not speak.

When I move the square and become the circle;
I will surround the horizon with an imaginary line
And the stars will become a triangulated pattern

That rebound inside human minds (before sleep arrives).

When the shape of imagination transforms;
I will see the patterns of motion and the graphs of time
Telling a story with a single line
That hasn't moved since formation.

To leave is to jump the gap between spaces
Yet [...] who has moved in two directions?
To stay is to jump the gap of time
Yet [...] who has spoken and remained silent?

So [...] I will reshape the mind
And change the view
And refigure the angles of the sea
I will change the degree (of my vision)
As I move through this spiral;
This motionless rise (and fall)
Into (and through) this — identity.

THE WIZARD

(129 lines)

Part I

When my sight falls into the underworld

Chaos will welcome my vision
And show me a world
Where disorder is the only law:
The ghost of the flesh
The self in the other
The shade on the moon rock
The mind of the body
The sight of emptiness
The dream of sleep
The other side of sound
Behind the conscious mind
Before time.

Chaos is the other side of order.

The clock ticks precisely each moment.
The space between ticks — sits precisely
Between each moment.

The clock hides chaos
Inside her mind;
And inside every mind
The other side looks
Through its own reflection.

> ### *Angel O*
> Everything has another side
> (Another side).

The line you draw — is the edge of your sight
The place you dwell — is the edge of your home.

The words you speak make oppositional sounds;
You are on the other side of your other side.

Stand on the razor's edge
Climb to the peaks of all thought mountains
And risk losing your mind;
For a slave won't have a mind to lose.
Besides [...] slave owners soon become slaves
To the descendants of their slaves.

Break free and find your own reflections:
Your own greatness
Your own sadness
Your own madness
Your own anger.

Kiss god on the forehead
Wipe away the tears
Look into your eyes and see yourself:

Such a young child.

Dear father god
Your order has another side.

Dear mother god
Your beauty has another side.

Dear child god
Your reflections have another side.

Dear fetus god
Your death will have another side.

Part II

Where do I go?
The other side is under
The other side is over.
Where do I stand?
Where do I look?

When my sight reaches above the expanse

Order will welcome my vision.
When my eyes open into the morning
Chaos will welcome me back.

The body of white light
The side inside the self
The brain of the mind
The inside of the void
The outside of the inside
The clarity of knowledge
The absence of emptiness
The search for Life!
The wakeful child playing with his fingers
Waiting for the other side to show itself.

> ### *Angel O*
> But the other side
> Will only show you herself
> When you are on her side
> And when you are on the other side (of the side you were on)
> You see another side
> And your center
> And your pendulum.

—

What was forbidden is now allowed
Music once hidden now has a sound.

Who tells me where to stand?
Who tells me to choose a side?

Angel O

To know the end of the story (before the middle)
Is to jump over yourself.
Don't miss the risk of being
The risk of being human.
A risk that brings fear
A risk that brings awe.
The risk of life
The risk of trust.

Part III

The fear traps my imagination
Inside prisons of authority;
A home with too many walls
A mind with not enough doors.

Angel O

But you need not fear more than you do;
The mind will release itself back into itself
For the mind can see both sides of itself.

There are no books or words that the mind can't discern
There are truths and lies on both sides
There are truths and lies in your own mind!
There are those who deceive and those who revive
There are things that you do and things that you hate
But the other side of yourself is another side of you.

The lines that you draw and the shapes that you make
They're erased and washed away
Moved aside and rearranged
You are on the other side

And you get to expand yourself

At your pace — in your speed.

—

I move through my dreams
And become my own imaginings.

I find my own language
And create another side.

For a moment
I contemplate
[…] […] […] […] […]
Kindness & Honesty — Joy & Pain
I stand on both sides
And breathe.

Part IV

When my sight falls into the underworld

Order will welcome my vision.
When my eyes climb over the expanse
Chaos will welcome me back.

When my life falls into forgetfulness
Breath will remind me of my home.

When my home fades into the unknown
This rock I think on
Will turn to stone
And sand
And smoke.

THE STORYTELLER

(40 lines)

There are no more words outside my eyes
There are no more gods inside my cries
There are no more stories around my mind.

Fear is made with words
Love is made with words:
Words for the sun
Words for the ray
Words for the tree
Words for the shade.

There are no more images before my thoughts
There are no more sounds behind my walls
There are no more signs — I seek no more.

Stories are not owned
    I have eyes.
Words are not owned
    I have ears.
Gods are not owned
    I have dreams.

> *Ancestor*
> *Who owns the ears?*
> *Who owns the eyes?*
> *Who owns your dreams?*

The other side of love is fantasy
The other side of peace is blame
The other side of trust is fear.

I look for trust — alone

I look for peace — in anger
I look for love — in separation.

There is no story to uphold
There are no last words that could be told
There are no actors without a mold

There is no perfect ending to this story.

The imagination
Moves around ideas.
Ideas hide. Words move.
Thoughts change.
Dreams end. Stories die.
And endings
Are soon forgotten.

Yet […] I tell my story for the future
With words that will reform.

THE REFORMER

(31 lines)

I asked: *What form can transform?*
For I didn't want to trap myself
Inside imagination.

I asked: *How many forms should I take?*
For I didn't know how to put anger inside peace
So […] I placed it with confusion.

And I placed playfulness in water
And I placed seriousness in fire
And I separated between sadness and joy
And between madness and order.

I asked: *Who will own the forms?*
For I wanted a center of return;
To look back from — to dream on
To leave from — and to turn to.

But I couldn't transform what I owned
So […] I lost myself in many forms.
I shatter in the night
And with the light
I am reborn.

I asked: *Who will see through the forms?*
For I knew continuity without beginning or end;
A voice that spoke over my thoughts
With stories and tales that I couldn't defend.

I asked: *What should I imagine?*
For I couldn't imagine a form which knows all forms
Although […] I could imagine a future which knows all pasts.

—

What I imagine will confirm itself.
What I think will appear.
What I am will be known.

So [...] I imagined — emptiness
And I felt whole.

THE PHILOSOPHER

(133 lines)

Part I

Before the knower
Before the known
Before the known could name its own absence
Before emptiness conceived of itself.

Before word
Before sound
Before thought
Before sight
Before light and space and time.

Part II

To know — is to separate:
This - knows - that.
To be this — is to be — not that.

Knowing is known
The unknown is — not even — unknown.
I know that I do not know the unknown.
How do I know?

Nothingness cannot exist.
If nothingness could exist — it would be something;
If there exists — in fact — nothing
I should not know to ask about it
But I know that I do not know
Therefore […] I ask: *Do I exist?*

An idea is something.

The concept - nothingness - is something.
What is nothing?
No thing is not.

—

Satisfy my longing eyes and
Show me what cannot be seen.

Part III

The unknown is not known:
The unknown is a concept of the known
The unknown is known through the known.

The limits of a concept
Are forever unknown;
When limits are seen
They expand.
When expansion sees what it never knew
The limits are seen
And they expand.

Existence exists!
Nonexistence exists as a concept within existence.

To know the unknown — is to create a new form;
If I must change it to know it
I never knew it.
Once it has gone — I see what it was;
But once it has gone — it never was.

Where is the edge of the known?

To acknowledge the unknown
Leaves the known unknown.
To ignore the unknown
Is to ignore the known.

Nothingness will not exist:
That which exists is known
That which does not exist
Is unknown to that which exists
And unknown to its own absence.

The known may know it does not know:
The unknown cannot know
That it cannot know.

To not know
Is to know awareness (mystical)
Yet […] not knowing — that I do not know — non-knowing.

Not a thought — not a feeling — not an action
Not movement — not stillness — not color
Not space — not sound — not sight
Not taste — not care — not indifference
Not silence — not darkness
Not not — not non.

Part IV

To know — is to perceive
To perceive — is to know.
To see — is to look
To look — is to see.

From awareness (mystical)
Absence is not known;
I know the absence of knowing
But if absence could know itself
It would not be itself.

A thing can only know itself
By looking at itself - with - itself.

To know the self — is to know knowing.
To not know the self — is to know not knowing!

Can I <u>know</u> the self — from <u>within</u> the self — <u>with</u> the self?

Perception is a reflection that imitates a thought
The mirror is a reflection that imitates image.
Either I am perception itself — or [...] I am perceived
Or [...] perhaps I am perception perceiving itself.

Knowing is to see what is — and unsee what was not;
I know I am known through reflections.

A thought enters into the known — from the unknown.
Sight sees from emptiness — and towards emptiness;
The sight which sees the <u>thing</u> — is not what it sees
The sight which sees <u>itself</u> — is not seeing a thing.

What I know — I am not.
What I am — I know not.

Part V

Emptiness is eternal
In absence;
It sees itself — but never is:
A nothing that knows something
A something that knows nothing.
A nothing that is known from something
A something that is known from nothing.

The unknown does not know itself.

That which knows it knows
Knows that it does not know.
What is — is in relation — to what it is not.

Nothing allows for something
Emptiness allows for existence
Unknowing allows for knowing
Awareness allows for silence
Death allows for life.

The self allows its own absence.
Emptiness allows its own absence.
Absence allows its own absence.
It allows its own absence.

The unknown is centerless
The known is the center.

I move through empty — space.

Part VI

Emptiness did not know Creation
For somethingness
Is no longer what it was once — not.

When the unknown becomes known
The known sees what it could not have known.
Hence [...] the known now knows

That **knowing** is not known
But a be-coming and be-going

And **unknowing** is a knowing
That only knows itself retrospectively.

Although the unknown cannot know itself
It has found eyes in the reflection
Of what - it - is not
And therefore becomes.

—
What absence is not — is what I am.
What I am — is what is not
What is not — is not known.

THE CREATOR

(62 lines)

Part I

Creation is a reshaping of the past
Into a molding for the future.

Continuity moves through itself
And sees itself through death
And into birth.

What is continuity?
What is eternity?
Where are beginnings?

That which created
Became a creation;
Coming and going
Arriving and leaving.

The birth of the new
Is the death of the old;
The birth of the young
Is the death of the old;
The old birth the young
The young bury the old;
Continuity moves through itself.

Extreme cold — extreme heat
Ice into fire — fire into water
From differences — a center is formed
In separation — a child is born.
Noticeable differences
Soon become unnoticeable

For the subject who is born
Is unknown to the object who has birthed.

Part II

What created the creator of creation?
There is no creation without a creator
Hence […] a creator is not the creation!
What can create without having been created?
All forms have a creator;
Absence of form — needs no creator.

If the creator is Not — and has No form:
Non-form created form!
What was not — became.
Hence […] form is existence
And absence of form does not exist
Thus […] a creator — of form — can/not exist.

Yet […]
Without a creator — creation is not.
I am. *Am I creation?*
Are we creators?

Where is the edge of our form?

What is — has a form
What is not — needs no form.
But what is not — soon becomes
And what becomes — is known to form.

Creation is the living threshold between
Known and Unknown. What was and what will be.
Continuity moves through itself with

A scrape

A spark
A puff of light
A tip
A wick
A glow
A face
A mouth
A voice
A word:

"Creation."

THE ACTOR

(38 lines)

Faces behind masks
Imitating sounds
Replicating motions
Embellishing details
Hiding inside the marrow of secrets.

I heard too much and not enough
I heard small deceptions producing solid truths
I heard dead authors teach lessons on immortality.

I saw a man without a beard
Holding a book about reincarnation.
I saw a woman without a dress
Holding a book about death.
I asked them: *How will it end?*
And I never saw them again.

I saw the elder behind a hologram
I saw children behind rehearsed minds

And I asked:
Why are we wearing our ancestor's skin?
Why are we carrying fermented spit?

> *Unknown Voice*
> Lies of shame and insecurity
> Lies of embarrassment and guilt
> Lies that show you your worth.

I molded my character with words
And created a moral compass
With the pendulum I found in suffering.

I molded my identity with a variety of thoughts
I fabricated — and told truths that hurt my heart
I lied — and moved the words surrounding words

But I told you what I could.

But after all — you should know:
There is no act — there is no stage
But strange contemplations
And presentations of the cage.

And after all — I should say:
I found no way — to tell the truth
Without editing this page.

I know my lines:
I am human! I am human! I am human!

THE HOST

(31 lines)

I have seen you scream at the birth of god
Why does birth hurt your womb?
Why does death punish your mind?
I have seen you pleasure yourself with pain
Whose name do you worship?
What did they engrave on your stone?

    From seed to blood
    From lust to mud
    My eyes have gone
    Where is the sky?
    The flesh will soon vanish from these bones
    Where are my eyes?
    Here once lived the known
    Who died without a body.

Have you reached the all-knowing?
Have you touched the unknown?

It remains
To be unknown.

Touch God's face
Lick God's thighs
You'll never see through God's eyes.
To see the unknown is
To remove your dilated pupils
And witness your own blindness!

Who has instructed me how to live?
Who has given me the pen and the word?
Who has provided the sounds of articulation?

The answers are found on the Gravestone:
    The one who died.
    The one who can't be seen.
    The one who can't be heard.

THE GHOST

(36 lines)

Head
Neck
Breath.
Where is my hand?
Where is my skull?

The **fingers** slip into my mind:
Grabbing the empty air.

A gold lightning rod vibrates in my belly
A broken hand feeds me raw earth;
I chew on mud and wipe it into my swollen eyes.

Uncovering an empty grave
I place my hands into the dirt
And breathe.

My **fingers** feel the pebbles in the earth
A rock is placed on top of my head;
It covers my ears
And holds me.

I am heavy.

We are safe.

The body is earth.
Flowers grow on the eyes
A tree grows on the chest
A thunderstorm of power
Rain [...] and deep pressure
Pulls the body deeper

Into the inner — crust
Of the earth.

—

Head is heavy.

I reach up — arms and hands and **fingers**
Through the thick earth
Until I can touch
The dense snow.
I climb out of the earth
And eat the ice.

It's cold
And **I am alive.**

THE ORPHAN

(20 lines)

Mother was born alone
Father was born alone
The child was born alone
They died alone.

When I am not
When you are not
When we are not.

Without a memory
Without a pencil
Without a mirror.

Brother was born alone
Sister was born alone
Lovers placed loneliness
Behind the tombstone.

The sky —
The earth —
The underworld —

The tears and sweat have dried
The light and warmth have died
— I found a friend within.

THE OUTCAST

(29 lines)

I said:
Where is my face?
Let me see the glory!

You said:
>One breath for our ears
>One sound for our voice
>One pen for our life.

You gave me your god
>I gave you my sin
You gave me your truth
>I gave you my life
You examined my shame
>I gave you my worth
You told me a story
>It punished my mind.

I was deceived
And went to sleep

And dreamt of
Gods afraid of humans
And humans afraid of ghosts;
A sun that hides from shadows
And a moon that absorbs the light.

**I ascended your mountain
— And touched its edge!**

I examined the shadows — and saw the sun
I looked inside the Holy of Holies: It was empty.

I examined the rituals — and bowed to the moon

And I saw the mask on your face
And the markings in your books.

THE STRANGER

(51 lines)

I don't know who held the strings — but it felt forced.

How do I move between this lifeless-living-skeletal-structure;
This directionless spiral — infinity O infinity?

When creativity arrives
I hear the relationships between sentences.

When fear arrives
I see all the other words.

I listen to false prophecies
I listen to true theories
But what's the difference?

I am troubled by silence.
I hear the emptiness echo […]
When I look for it — it disappears
When I try to see it — I hear it
When I try to hear it — I see it.

I get caught up inside it
And forget why I started
Or who it turned me into.

I am caught up inside it
And it is caught up in me;
We are simply releasing it
Articulating it
Amplifying it

Then leaving it alone.

—

I went to look for self
I went to look for you
I went to look for it
I never returned.

Life is not what I thought it was;
The mind doesn't care to distinguish
The heart doesn't think a breath
The clock loves pleasure and hates pain
And the calendar is indifferent.

The greatest fear is:
    What if it controls me?
The greatest high is:
    What if I am free?

But it arrives when it arrives
And it leaves when it leaves.

I don't know who held the strings.
They said: Go this way.
They said: No — not that way.
They said: Fuck you.
They said: You are a sinner.
They said: You can't do it.

I said: No.
    I know I can't do it
    But I am doing it.

They said: Go to sleep.

I said: No.
    This is too strange.

THE CHILD

(36 lines)

If I am as I am: *Who am I?*
And if I am not as I seem: *What am I?*
Who are my ancestors?
Where is my voice?

I asked these questions.

I stood between the mirrors
Of pleasure and pain
I asked my questions
But nobody came.

I stood naked in front of the ark
And climbed through the curtain;
Through the fireproof doors
I put my ears inside the scroll
And drowned into the absorbing ink.

I asked:
Who has inseminated humanity?
Who birthed the mind?

Where is the mother?
Who is the father?

I asked the prophets:
Where is my voice?
I asked the homeless:
Where is my home?
I asked the children:
Who is in charge?

I crawled deeper underground
And unleashed   Voice!   Voice!   Voice!
But I heard the screams
Rebounding off my throat.

I waited to see
But my sight hadn't changed
I waited to listen
But it sounded the same.

Questions and answers
Whispers and secrets
Pleasure and pain.

THE CAREGIVER

(54 lines)

Part I

I followed the smoke to its source
And discovered disguised mothers
Who revise stories
When the flames of fear
Grow too big to conceal.

I asked Mother Nature:
Who is your lover?
I asked Father Sky:
Where is your tongue?

My lover is sleeping
My tongue is bleeding
I kissed the mad spider
And lit a fire under the table.

I removed the floorboards
And swept the dust into the ocean.

I took the paintings off the wall
And put them into a potion
I found in my grandfather's suitcase;
He kept it to preserve his memories.

I removed my shoes
And my raincoat
And my hair.

I removed the mirrors from the hallway
And burnt the harmonium.

I broke the windows
And put the glass in a bag
And put the bag in his grave.

Part II

They told us to build gates around gates;
But we never found the gates
And you stopped searching
When you saw the guards blindfolding our eyes;
That was the last time you looked into the deceptive river.

We never told you what we thought
We never told you what we saw.

We saw good children
And hurt children
And sad children
And mad children.

We saw some people standing in the back row
We saw one person sitting on a throne
We saw three old men surrounding the king
We saw the queen hiding behind the curtain
We saw the search come to an end
We saw orphans without shoelaces
And leaders without pens.

We never told you what we learned
We never told you what we heard.

We heard him moan before he died
We heard her scream after she cried
We heard them laughing at the poor
We heard you underneath the floor
We couldn't walk

We couldn't talk

We told you what we could.

THE SEEKER

(29 lines)

I seek — hold eternity forever
I seek — find the perfect spiral
I seek — discover the perfect mystery
I seek — uncover the endless future

And the unknown disappears behind me.

Motions of thought
Circle the circumference
Of a mind that can't find its own origin.

Sight disappears behind me
Light reappears before me
Time moves from inside me
And motion brings me through.

I don't know what I seek
For I seek what can't be found.

I seek — know the unknown
I seek — capture motion
I seek — hold time
I seek — grasp emptiness
I seek — see blindness
I seek — hear the voice that has never spoken.

—

So […] the seeker must seek what cannot be found
Uncover a light one cannot uncover
Before **seeing** what could not have been;
And **unseeing** what had once been seen.

And a seeker must seek and uncover deceit

Before the eyes are given sight
Before the movement is given feet
Before the words are formed in speech.

And the future sees what the past could not have perceived.

THE PROPHET

(408 lines)

Part I

I ask: *Where is nature?*
I ask: *Who is God?*
I ask: *Why am I?*

I confront the absolute
And expose an endless root:

The silence that never speaks
The voice that won't submit
The seas that have no mercy
The skies that have no home
The light that won't ignore
This shadow in her view.

Nurture won't submit to reason
Nature won't submit to law.

Will silence respond to reason?
Will order reason with chaos?
Who will respond to suffering?
Will I respond to my suffering?

Nature — **Nurture** — *are we not* **Natural?**
Where did I acquire my reasons?

We rip the brain in half
To see and understand

Have we understood?
Who has stood under?

We have shelters in space
We have cities in water
We are kind and we are cruel
We are strong and we are weak
We have hospitals for the body
We have libraries for the mind
We heal the sick
We kill the healthy
We imprison the orphan
We breed the heretic
We hide the truth
We birth fear into newborns
We build prisons for safety
We blame the healthy for dying
We blame the sick for living
We blame death for dying
We have nothing to blame!

Who will we blame?

Voice
No doctor can save you from death
No mystic can give you your breath
No teacher can save you from yourself.

We read our poems with the blood of reason
But we have forgotten how to feel.

We sacrifice our life for understanding;
Yet every book has a beginning
And every author has an end.

Part II

I seek objectivity
And find solitude.

Where is the object of my agreement!

I say: Let me fight for the truth
But I lose it every night.
I seek the right way
And find conflicting sides.

So […] I say: Let me confront the absolute.

Some voices tell me to do everything
Some voices tell me to do nothing
Some say: Leave.
Some say: Stay.
Some voices tell me to hide
Some voices tell me to lie
Some voices don't speak.
Some voices say: Continue in your way
Uncover who you are
Look into this divine conflict!

But I have encountered lies — stories
Fairy tales — told to children
Told to children — and the children
Tell more children — and children
Become adults — and adults have learned to lie
And lies become gossip — and gossip becomes the truth
And the truth becomes the fight.

And the truth stands on top-most-high — vibrating:
                    J-U-S-T-I-C-E
—
Show me a justice that can see without eyes
Show me a truth that can see every side.

The law follows justice
And the people follow the law.

What is justice?
What is law?

Law is formed with observation
And observation is formed with reason
And reason is formed with language
And language forms the right and the wrong
And persuasive expression is power.

Power molds the majority
With the flames of fear
And the fumes of hope.
Power listens to the majority
Through the eyes of poverty
And the ears of gold.
Power defines morality
With persuasion.

Authority is made with an image;
Power molds the dream of the will
Power is a force fighting on every side
Power forms and destroys
Power is given to

The Judge — who must equally describe all sides
And decide if justice is fair!

—

If the judge is impartial
How will ze decide?
Who is the judge of morality?

Did she encounter Justice
Or her own Mercy?

Did he encounter Mercy
Or his own Justice?

Does justice have a side?
Will we choose life or death?
Who is the judge of all judges?
Where does their mercy belong?
Where does the absolute reside?

Voice
I am the judge of my inner thoughts
I favor myself in the way that I do
I punish myself in the way that I do.

Part III

Are we to be judged by taste?
Are we to be counted like coins?
Are we to be slaughtered in shame?

How many perspectives are there?
Rationality has left me seeking madness
And reason disappears behind shadows of doubt.

Who speaks the verdict?
If the judge follows wealth — *who owns justice?*
If the judge follows power — *who knows justice?*
If the judge follows truth — *who sees justice?*

If the judge follows law
And law follows reason
What is the reason?

If predictability is predictable — *why have choice?*
Without choice — *why have reason?*
Without reason — *what is law?*
If the judge follows reason
And reason follows its own trail
And patterns shift with improved reasoning

What is justice?

If the judge follows god
How will you persuade without reason?

If the law can be persuaded to change
Reason is justice!
If the law can't be persuaded to change
Reason is unreasonable.

If justice is reason
And reason reforms
What is history?
Also: *Where exactly are we going?*

—

Tell me — specifically
What does your utopia look like?
What does your enlightenment look like?
Who does your Moshiach look like?
Like you — it looks like you and your people.

> ### *Voice*
> *Will the world submit to your vision?*
> *Will war bring you your outcome?*
> *Or is war the effect you seek?*

How can relativity judge the whole?
What justification have you found — that allows you
To stand face-to-face — before life and death
And refrain from asking: Why!

On what basis does the judge declare the verdict: Thou Shalt Not?
The law of the people!
Who has named the judge: Your Honor?
The law of the people!
Is justice not revenge?

What is revenge?

We measure our law with rulers and numbers
         — Kings and Queens and sticks
Who gave us human ownership?
Who engraved numbers on our skin?
Who made the perfect stick length?
The law of the people!
And the people fight for a ruler.

What measurement is free from bias?

We favor one and disregard the other
We find beauty in the eye
We lose tears over love
Slaves acquire the children of their owners
Leaders are soon exposed as human:
How disappointed we are.

—

How do I measure justice if I have nothing to measure it against?
Justice is the measurement of measurements!
But who owns justice?
Each day brings new information

And with new information;
A change of mind and form.

And I am left readjusting the holy scales of the mind.

Who resets the scales?

Perspectives shift and move between ideas.
Justice is alive!
Justice is the will of the people
But where is the will of the people?
Where are the scales?

Who sees justice?

Justice asks us for our will
And the people obey the masters;
They draw a map from firewood
And hang it behind the pages of the book.

> ### *Voice*
> Without a soul — the eyes are blind to life
> Without a map — the fearful are lost.

Why do we draw our maps with circles?

We found safety — but we lost freedom
We sought freedom — but we found terror.

> ### *Voice*
> I need not obey the mind nor the heart.
> I am the measurement!
> I am the compass.

—
With what do I measure justice?

On the holy scales!
We declare our master and mistress
We declare good and evil; a winner and a loser.
We have given justice our — eyes
Covered them with — words
Stories — and cloth — and rage
But we can't forget what we have chosen to ignore.

We hide the scales and disregard
The welder and the poet.

> ### *Voice*
> Hide inside the pages of mortality.

Only the high priest can adjust lifeless scales
But the high priest died in silence.

We vote — we ask questions
We dialogue — we reason with law
Yet [...] we have scales — we have water!

On whose authority are ideas heard?
Who owns measurement?

Who knows all perspectives?
And if I could know all perspectives
Would I speak at all!

Part IV

The mind has turned stiff-cold (and secretive).
Who has allowed the heart to speak falsely?
We favor our own people and refuse to acknowledge <u>our</u> self.
We think new thoughts — but stop before the end.

Each god has a chosen people
And people have a chosen god
A chosen people — a better way
A better goddess. A secret god.
Are we chosen for our worth?
Are we chosen for our work?

Our books have created justice
For their time — but their time is not ours.
And justice has become blind to our future.

Justice has no taste
Justice has no scales.
Justice has reason without meaning
And meaning without words.

Justice is indifferent:
Justice is guilty of innocence.

The lion's jaw locks — blood is drawn
And hunger is satisfied by death.
Life is killed by the living.
Justice is alive!

What human dares look into the absolute?
A human who wants to retain the heart!

Distinction allows for sight
And the taste buds of the tongue-mind
Relativity enhances pleasure and pain
Perspective births experience
And experience broadens understanding
And understanding is thought combinations
Which surgically transform themselves
With blades of fear and dreams of hope.

I fear understanding
And once I understand — I fear becoming.
I fear adulthood
Wounded by separation — I fear the other side.
I fear balance
Removing the branches — I lose my drive to uncover myself.

How could I go on?

Yet […] the air of worth
Moves through my center
And I uncover the mind of justice
And I uncover my own blindness.

I see where I am
I am here:

With measurements and numbers
With thoughts and moments
With the others.

We are here with each other.

Have we not tortured ourselves enough?
Our lies have become too fragile;
They are killing the dreams we once imagined.

We have lost ourselves in the story;
Our imaginations have developed thoughts of reason
And our dreams have become too real to wake from.

Please take off the blindfolds from Lady Justice
Please uncover the ark and expose the naked scroll
Please let us be human and we will allow — **reality.**

Lies have created lies
Stories have hypnotized our will.

We have finally believed — but we have forgotten belief!
We started running — but forgot where we were going.
We have long past our prophecies
And our **fantasy** has a voice we can't **reason** with.

—

I have an identity that molds itself.
I am forced between pleasure and pain

After all — I should say:
Here is an abstract structure — which enables identity to live
Between known and unknown
Between pleasure and pain
Between thought and feeling
Between self and other
This is our **humanity!**

The human can't own justice
For the human is identity
And identity asks justice to justify its own existence.

What am I afraid of justifying to myself?
What am I afraid of knowing?

There is no justice without perspective
There is no perspective without understanding
There is no understanding without forgetfulness.

Who can live as one?
Judge – defender – prosecutor – victim – juror – witness – executioner.

Only a criminal can be a true judge of crime
But who wants a thief and a liar sitting on the throne?
Who wants to hear the heretic's description of god?

But perhaps there are those who wish to listen to everything
Over the sun — between the moon — and under the sea.

All that is and isn't — is what it is — and isn't what it's not.

Open your ears to the liar and you might hear justice speaking
Open your hands to the thief and you might see justice stealing
Open your mind to the heretic and you might glimpse justice thinking!

Part V

I will judge
Observe and conclude:
Justice is alive.

Justice needs no verdict
Justice moves with time
Justice will never rest.

The law must turn and face the **living** child.

Law has held us imprisoned
To a vision — disappeared.
Laws change. People leave.

The view soon evaporates.

Justice is a heartbeat
Justice is seen.

I move through the unknown
I move through the known;
Let me not bow to greatness
Let me bow to the heart
Let me bow to life.

Let me open my eyes

When it feels alive — let me bow
When it suffers inside — let me bow.

Let my heart bow in all directions
Let me bow from the solitude of mind.
We need not lose our hearts
We need not lose our minds
We need not bow to the unknown
We need not bow at all.

We may retain our heart
We may praise our world.

> ### _Voice_
> Be with your Will and your Will will be with you.
> You need not give your Will.
> Rather [...] give your ear — then your voice!

I don't understand what I haven't yet uncovered
But I need not sell my soul to the words behind thoughts
I remain human — I am left with the question
I conceive compassion and revive love
In my private mind-heart.

I need not sell death to an afterlife
I bow to death — but vow to life.
I live my life knowing and forgetting
As I am uncovered by the unknown.

When life arrives
    I will be honest
When death arrives
    I will be kind.

The deeper I go into time
The more there is to see;
Old theories fall away
As new children come to be.

But who will be the seers of justice?
A molding she was — a symbol she is.
Who dares unveil the blindfold
And expose her lifeless eyes?
Only justice!
Who dares uncover the grave of the prophet
And expose his lifeless bones?
Only justice!
Who dares disclose the holy book
And expose the thoughts of humanity?
Only justice!

Who is the judge of your body and mind?
Who owns your feelings?
How will you navigate yourself?

How will you measure your life?

Listen — hear — and foresee:
Nature is Nurture and Nurture is Nature
Understand what we don't understand!
We rise above where we once stood
We are the children of the scale.

Frightening. Worthy. Life.

—

What am I to do with this confrontation?
How am I to travel back in time?
Before the poets wrote the word
Before the welders molded the scale
Before the carpenters built the ark
Before the mathematicians divided worth.

I confront justice
I am confronted in time
I confront myself within!

I need not mold an image
Nor shape a dream of fear
I will find a way through the many ways.

—

Is justice not within perspective?
Don't we all hear the earth's heartbeat?
My vision is the judge of what it sees
My thoughts think themselves to sleep
I draw my maps and think my thoughts

This light is true sight
This sound is true sound.

THE MASTER

Do not fear the edge of the razor
Do not fear the eyes of your master
Do not fear the doors of perception
Do not fear the high mountain
Do not fear madness
Do not fear
Do not fear
Do not fear your mind:

Your head is resting in — hands
See through top of — skull
Kiss brain — kiss head
Do not fear closeness.

Do not fear the mind of god
Do not fear the eye of truth
Do not fear the words of reflection:

Go higher yet
Climb into the highest
Fall into the lowest.

Do not fear your thought
Do not fear loyalty
Do not fear betrayal
Do not fear the lips that lie
Do not fear the tongues of truth
Do not fear
Do not fear
Do not fear your way:

Melt into disobedience

With blades of thought
And arrows gathered from dishonest teachings;
Throw them swiftly with your speech
And pierce the deceptive mind with your pen.

Do not fear
There is no home for travelers
Do not fear
There is no home for outcasts
Do not fear the emptiness
For you sit in the **Holy of Holies.**

Do not fear El-Ohim
Do not fear El-Shaddai
Do not fear Mother Earth
Do not fear Father Sky
Do not fear Winds of birth
Do not fear Names of death
Do not fear Gods of gods
Do not fear Hollow shell
Do not fear Talking tongues

Do not fear to stand between
Creation and destruction.

Do not fear
Do not fear
Do not fear to know the known

Do not fear the void.

THE WANDERER

(26 lines)

When it moves my hand
Write in this wind
When it has my back
Rest in this wind
When it pulls my head
Fly in this wind
When it drags my feet
Crawl in this wind
When it holds my breath
Swim in this wind
When it takes my form
Sleep in this wind
When it chains my soul
Bow in this wind
When it grabs my thought
Suffer in this wind
When it freezes my water
Shiver in this wind
When it burns my wick
Sweat in this wind
When it turns my heart
Dance in this wind
When it opens my mind
Submit in this wind
When it divides my time
Love in this wind.

THE ARTIST

(33 lines)

I have heard the screams of the past
I have felt the dreams of the future
I have seen the eyes of the mind
I have been born to move through
And I have nowhere left to hide.

The earth is moving
The moon is moving
The sea is moving
Thoughts are moving
Blood is moving
Sound is moving
Simultaneously
Moving.

I can't keep up
I can't give in;
To keep up — is to go to war
To give in — is to lose the war.
To keep up — I must fight for a cause
To give in — I must die for one.

Fuck   You

I will live — in between.

Day and night — in between.
I will be — in between
The sea and the land
The ink and my pen

I will live — in between.

I will swim in the storms
I will sleep in the hills
I will move with the wind
I will change every thought.

Where else am I to go?
What else am I to know?
Who else am I to be?

THE ANCESTOR

(44 lines)

Who is the god of worth?

The mind is worthy of thought
The thought is worthy of word
The word is worthy of speech
The pallet is worthy of taste
The fingers are worthy of touch
The heart is worthy of warmth.

Who is worthy of worth?

What I see — is seen
What I know — is known
What is unknown — is unknown.

Where is worth located?

There is no savior inside the ocean
There is no rope between the sky
There is no Moshiach outside the heart
There are no owners of the mind
There are no masters of immortality
Worth is alive. Worth is alive.

Every hand is worthy
Every body is worthy
Every mind is worthy
Every breath is worthy.

—

I speak words that comfort my ears
With worth silencing emptiness
With worth arousing breath.

My words are just like yours:
In honesty and kindness
In doubt and fear
In greatness and criticism
Inspired and alone.

My worth is just like yours:
Skin — tears — sound
Structured bones
Rebounding tones
Blood flows
Neurons glowing
Atoms — cells
Nerves and laughter.
Just like yours.

On whose authority do I speak?

This voice that makes sound
These fingers that hold the pen.

Worthy are ears to hear
Worthy are lips to kiss.

THE MONSTER

(24 lines)

When the fear arises — do not fear this fear
Rearrange it — until it speaks of peace.

I listen to it — inside fear — I can hear
So [...] I listen.

I fear the rearrangement of insight.

Fear. It is real. Fear before birth.
Words. They create. They destroy.

I listen and hear:
    The fear of **art**
    The fear of **self**
    The fear of **sight**
    The fear of **peace**
    The fear of **power**
    The fear of **thought**
    The fear of **madness**
    The fear of **mortality**
    The fear of **awareness.**

To own a person is to lose your Self.
To own a thought is to lose your Mind.

> ### *Clown X*
> To look away is to hide
> To escape understanding is to lie
> To believe all wisdom is to die.

I rearrange it — until it speaks of peace
And sometimes it rearranges me.

THE WITNESS

(71 lines)

I don't remember
What I've forgotten
I don't remember who I was
Or where I was going.

I don't remember being born
Into the explosion of life
Or when my back and neck were formed.

I don't remember moving my fingers
Or bending my bones.

I don't remember my skull — expanding
I don't remember my mind — broadening
I don't remember my neck — transforming.

I don't remember what to trust
I don't remember what to fear
I don't remember what to say
I don't remember.

The mind woke up
The blood in my feet
And sparks shot down my spine
And flashed into my speech.

It was dark before
I woke up.

—

My cheeks were swollen
And my eyes were in pain
I had been born into shame;

Fingers without speech
Thoughts without sound
Words without ink.

I don't remember
I had no memory before it began.

I heard collective memories
Climbing into my ears:
Memories in my gut
Words fighting
In my head. Heads. Head.
Distant memories fading from an image
Close memories that hurt my forehead
Lost memories that I will not recall
Memories that search for themselves
Memories that laugh in time
Memories that play between lines.

But I found a note in the ocean
And read it when no one was around.

It said:
   I searched for the heavens
   Until my eyeballs were bare
   And my eyelids were torn;
   Burned by the sun
   And torn by my hands:
   My eyes were worn.

   My worth had been taken hostage
   By honest prophets with honest words
   And guides who spoke honest lies
   Before asking me to take out my own eyes.

   It was never supposed to go this way

Something felt wrong.

I spoke to my dreams and whispered promises
I hummed soft tunes to the almighty
In my dreams
And my dreams were strong
And my song was patient.

When I died
I had no face left to remember
But I remember — I remember
I remember how cold it was.

[end of note]

I don't remember why.
I don't remember.
But I remember this:
I was in love with truth
And the absolute
Exposed its roots.

THE GUARDIAN

(58 lines)

Where do you hide?
Where have I found myself?
Where is the secret mind?

When you are in your solitude

Am I yours?
Are we blind?
Should I trust you?
Are you mine?

I don't want control
My obsessions are whole
Please allow me to explain:
I've come from the underground
Where the soft light burns my eyelids
And pleasurable lines lick at my eyes.

I have feelings that haunt me.

I don't mean to touch your scars
But I must have you understand
What I can't yet explain.

Please hear me!
Please see me!

I grow inside regression
I fight to kill deception
I am right here by your side;
Hiding behind insecurities
(I am sorry).

My insecurities fit inside your hidden gloves
And I ask if I am loved.
Completely loved.
Lonely love.

I am strong enough to face the fear — near
And investigate this most dangerous mirror
Nearer...nearer... it screams in me: Nearer!

Did I kiss her eyes?
Did you kiss her when she cried?

How lovers love to test their mind
Draw their jealous seed and spit
Into the fertile stomach pit
Of insecurity and fear.

The mud of the mind splatters
Through vision. Becoming one
The one — the only one.

And I am left - alone - to explore
Love through the fears of my imagination.

—

Love wounds and heals
It hurts — it feels real
It confuses the thoughtful.

Separation is love
Separation hurts
Separation is creation
Creation is variation
Variation is distinctiveness
Distinctiveness is separation
Separation is return
Separation is awareness.

—

Let me turn around to see myself
Let me turn within to know myself
Let me turn away to find myself

For I must go alone and approach myself.

I hear begging lips
Slip into the history
Of past intimacy
To sing wounding love songs.

But my heart hurts
And my ears have
Submitted to the screams
Of the one who hid behind
The mirrors of fear

And the voices of rejection
(rejection...rejection...rejection).

—

I heard you in my ears — saying:
 Worship my madness
 My sadness — please
 Worship my head
 Worship my spine
 Worship my sole
 Remove the crust around my eyes
 Touch my tongue
 Dust my heart
 Worship my soul.

 Don't run away
 Please don't run away
 Please don't be afraid.

And I replied:
I can't run away
For I can't gather my thoughts

When I am - pushed - into a corner
And asked to choose
Over and under

And I can't uncover my outgoing breath
When I am submerged into salt water
And asked to describe the heart
In color and space and sound.

Your imagination holds my image
Inside mind — out of time.

I - also - imagine myself
I - also - have an image
And I can't imagine the ending.

It may be the image of the imagination
That has — turned humans into ghosts
With gods who boast:
Look at me — look at me — look at me
But I only see myself.

And when I look away
I see you staring at me.

—

I heard you in my neck — saying:
    As you gaze into my mirrored eyes
    Longing for yourself
    You might catch a small reflection.
    Don't blame me for your own discovery
    For I can only be the other
    I too was made in the image
    Of your imaginings.

    Why love! — why pain!
    Don't hurt my worshiped name!

We are not the same
We must hold our own shame.

So [...] we spoke together — saying:
Our wounds have similar names
Our memories hide behind the same stories
Our descriptions and restrictions
Have emerged from the same scriptures
We were both buried alive
And born as ghosts who defend broken gods.

When we dreamt of life — we uncovered the dead
And the literature that we read
And the voices in our head
And the empty neglect
That vacuumed our life out
From the belly of poisonous memories
And showed us regret
And showed us the nightmares
And patterns that entangled
Our deep-needed rest
Forever in debt
To guilt and shame we loathe and detest
And yet [...]

Our wounds have shared a story
And our eyes have seen the broken
And our ears have heard

The pitch of loneliness   0 0 0 0 0

We have played together in the dark
We have seen behind the heart
We have begged to be unleashed
We have been pushed into the ground;
They stepped on our eyes

They put us inside
Volcanic lava
Red-black-silver-gold
They molded our sight
Into old concrete stone
Liquid bone
We moaned alone as
They spat on our throne.

We called for you
But it was too late.

—

And I heard you in my knees — saying:
    I saw the whips slash the skin of your heart
    And with the broken fragments of cries
    I heard your echoes in the empty skies
    I asked again — and again — but you already know
    The shameful slap that silence gave me.

And we spoke together again — saying:
We have been consumed by the aesthetics of death's perfume
We bloom — yet
We never reach
The end.

We are broken
We are broken
They are broken — forever.

Our image is shattered
Our mirrors reflect in too many directions.

Our love — our pain
Our worshiped fame
Our hidden blame
We are the same

We haven't gone wrong
We were always the same.

Our love — our pain
We haven't gone wrong
We each have our own way
We each have our own name.

THE SKEPTIC

(66 lines)

The self — trusts other
The self — trusts itself
The self — trusts the mistrust of the other
The self — trusts the mistrust of itself.

When I trust in another
It is - I - who trusts.

When I mistrust myself and call for — the other
I trust myself to trust the other.

If you tell me to distrust myself
Why should I trust you?
Only to have you guide me through myself
And trust your distrust of me?

I distrust your direction
And would rather trust the mistrust in myself
Then trust your distrust — of me.

If you tell me to trust myself

I trust you.

If I can't trust myself
If I am a liar to myself
If I trust the other over myself;
It is - I – who's trusting myself to trust the other.

If I know my lie — I know my honesty!
If I can't trust myself — I can't trust the other;
For I cannot trust myself to trust the other.

If you ask me to trust a book <u>over</u> myself
It will be - I - who reads the book.
If you tell me <u>how</u> to perceive the book
It will be <u>you</u> who I experience
(I want to encounter the book).

If you ask me to trust another over myself;
If the other deceives me
And leads me away
I might never know.

Yet [...] If I deceive myself
I am the deceiver and the deceived.
If dishonesty enters from me
I can navigate back to my beginning.

But if you are dishonest to me
And I follow in your truth
Long after your death
I would have lived life
Suffocating on your word.

I don't know if you are being honest
I know my sensations
I know how honesty tastes
And how it moves.

The self is always with me
There is-no-way out
There is-no-way in.
I walk alone
Through
Myself
And trust that I am here.

—

I listen to the inner dialogues

I don't trust words or thoughts;
I speak words and think thoughts
I feel feelings and think words.

I trust trust
I trust doubt
I trust life
I trust spirit
I trust death
I trust sensation
I trust that I am trusting
I trust that I am who I am.

And I will be who I was — when I was — what I was.

THE LOVER

(73 lines)

Thoughts communicate — the body receives
Speech has a release which the mind conceives
Eyes look into each other and speak
What is not said is seen.

Artists hold each other in abstraction

Closer — closer — let's move closer
Into the other side of shame
Where worth lusts to touch
The soft lips of pleasure and pain.

—

My face is wet
My heart is deep inside
And my tongue longs to taste
Your gentle soul
And kiss your eye sockets.

—

I watch your lips
Fall from your face
And into my mouth;
I can taste your disguise
As I move through your thighs
And enter inside
Where you
Undress your wild flames
Before my eyes
And expose your hunger for eruption.

—

I want to speak to you
I want to see into you
I want to move with you

I want to come through you.

—

Your body is warm
Your mind is wet
Your words are true
Your face is soft
Your lips
Are not my lips
And your [...]
Kiss is strange
Your tongue is sweet
Your eyes are bright
Your skin and hips
Hover — as my image
Falls away from itself.

Your fragrance reminds my mind.

—

I write my ink
On your lips
And in your wild howl
I submit to your call.

I worship — I do.
Please touch me with your soul
Whole — whole — my role [...]

Our moving bodies — stop!

Through the waves
Into the sea
To explode with the ocean of
Liquid
Salt
Silver
Black

Volcanic lava.

We are set
To forget
We existed
We exist [...]
We remember
We remember
Remember
Remember
We arrive at our longing
For a moment
For a moment
For a moment.

Lay peacefully
Hold gently —
As we fall back into our self.

THE PAINTER

(26 lines)

The canvas moved inside the earth
As I observed the world we made
The spirit landed on my shoulder
Her ink dripped on this page.

I drew the story of life — with lines and circles
Before I walked away.

I drew the outline of my hands on her face
I threw the paint on her scars
And knew she would taste
The drawing behind every line.

I took the graphite out the pencil
And the hairs out from the brush
I took my fingers off my hands
And my words off my tongue
I took my soul out from the ground
And put it inside her bones
I drew the outline of my heart
On the inline of her spine.

I turned my candle upside down
And my pencil downside up
I reversed the order of our rearrangement
And used the wax to draw what I heard.

I wrote the words and smoked the herb
Until I calculated earth.

I drew her breasts and drank her milk
Until I heard our love at rest.

THE MADMAN

I perceive my eye
Looking at itself
Through a reflection
And I forget which eye is seeing
And which eye is seen.

I heard a voice that said:
    Speak - your - mind.
    Speak - your - stomach - in - your - speech.

    The daggers that were thrown at your head
    Are blades of breath that have no mouth.
    The arrows that poisoned your mind
    Are blades of love that have no lips.

    The words that locked your ears between steel plates of fears
    Are pockets of air looking for sound
    Word and breath.

    And then they pass away.
    And then they disappear.

—

I place my heart
Behind my rib cage
And touch my chest with my hands.

I breathe into my heart
My walls expand each breath
The expanse contracts

I inhale the view
And fall into the horizon.

I move down my ribcage
Up my spine
Behind my eyes.

And behold I see:

The earth moving between the sun and the moon
The lizard with a story for my heart
The mirror with an image for my eye
The tree with a branch for my head.

And behold I hear:

The spider crawling between the walls
The spiral moving
The clock spinning
The calendar turning
The compass clicking into place.

And behold I know:

The color white and the color black
The blue sky and the green grass
The taste of cloves
The smell of olives
The oil of love.

And behold:

My eye returns from the mirror
With water on my spine
And color
And paint
In my speech.

THE HERETIC

I look inside
The inferno of my heart;
Another dive through
The red-silver-hot-liquid lava:

It enters through my eyes
And - burns - through my mind
Until the thoughts gather the strength to
Confront the - face - of the absolute
And question the existence of death.

My lungs beg for — one last breath
My eyes grab for light — one last glimpse at life

— But it's gone now.

Why do I go into the fires?
*Why am I so compassionate to doub*t?

I bring back rocks with engravings;
Petroglyphs of consciousness
Sentences of words — gathered
From the rays of creation
From the underworld of suffering
From kind people — and hurt people
From the sky — and from the quest;
Which has me daydreaming about
The strings of madness
And the limitations of reason.

I go into the fires to learn about pain;
I return with an indifference that comforts.

These uncontrolled fires of the heart
Have taught me who I am not;
They burned through my eyelids
And I couldn't look away.

I received potential
I provided my seed
I placed my soul between madness and meaning
I saw where discernment is calculated
Where the heart and mind unite
Where trust and doubt balance.

> *The Speaker*
> *Navigating potential*
> *Without a map?*
> *Navigating the underworld*
> *Without a compass?*

The map is my breath
The compass is the will.

—

When it's time to fly
I'll gather myself
And fly into the sun
Where abundance seeks
Its own reflections.

When it's time to be alone
I will know — there were others
Who saw the cruelty (forgiveness)
And remained kind.

And […]

When it's time to die
I will hold the heart

And release my breath into the question

Of all questions.

THE HERO

(38 lines)

The truth - stops - the blood
From rising through
The arteries — in the neck.

Hungry for blood — the brain panics.

—
I place the truth into a worn-out slingshot
And shoot it through holy books
Which throw my words towards
The never-ending-lava-fire-falls
That swallow dreams
With water and ash
Water and ash.

I am to decide
To choose a side — to put aside
But I am caught inside
The flames and gases of opposition.

My ears seek comfort
But a dozen frozen teeth appear
And bite at my eyes
And frostbitten lips
Begin to spit arrows
Past my chest
Through my ribs
And into the heart of all my love.

The shock vibrates
The center moves

This - - **trembling** - - holy place!

My hands panic
My arms shiver
My face — shaking.

—

I lower my head into darkness
And lift out the heart of the heart.

I pull the arrows with my hand
Heal the wounds with my tongue
Kiss the scars with my lips

Relieve the thoughts with my words.

And the blood flows again
And comfort returns to absorb the thoughts

And I am content.

THE FIGHTER

What was I to do about a truth
Implanted through me in youth?
Must I - fight - a war that was never mine?
I have been born in your time
But who am I?

Perhaps not a warrior
But a worrier — a sufferer
I look into the eyes of emptiness
And see inside the coffins of forgetfulness.

So often I am afraid of myself.

I saw prophets lead children
Into the graves of guilt;
Too afraid to touch the bones themselves
They deceive the young with loving lies.

Holy books to defend?
Frightened small children running in circles
Wide eyes — lighting fires
Lighting fires in the heart
With sticks
Sticks and rocks
Fearful rage-filled angry gods
Tears — tears — tearful fears
They scream so loud
They look so sad

They say:
> **Remember your name**
> **Remember your shame!**

But this war was never mine!

I have been sentenced
To gaze at life
To climb the hill
To push the rock
To spit out blood
To cry until — laughter
To laugh until — pain.

I see movement and I am afraid
I see them dancing and I am ashamed
I see sadness surround the earth
I see empty skies and vanishing storms;
They seem so distant and unfamiliar.

I move faster
As the screams begin
And the truth sinks in
And the body and mind fall apart.

And I feel the strings of language
Being pulled through my lips.

And I stop!

You have been born on earth
You have been birthed by will

There is no fight to lose
There is no fight for you.

THE MEDIATOR

(56 lines)

It moves through
Breath
To test
The resistance
Of boundary.

Small pockets of air
leap through my eyes
To look back at me.

I stare and look away.

I have learned from the heart:
Chaos loves to move between structure
And structure gets excited by the breeze.

My boundary expands with vision
And I create an entrance into the unknown
And an exit back home to the center of breath.

My walkway has been formed in resistance.
Resistance that allows me to see through myself
As I move **between** the image patterns
Where the **boundaries** are unrecognized.

I walk between walls and taste the ink of memory
I talk to the walls and write letters on the floor
I open windows and walk through doors;
These windows reflect delusion
These doors cause confusion.

Walking through the walls of fear

Into the other side — of the other side.

—

She seduces my heart with her
Breath — and her
Eyes — and her
Teeth — and her
Lips. Her lips.
Our elbows bend — and our thoughts
See behind the reflection: Words:
We play within our limits
We reach beyond them
We expand our understanding
Of madness and prophecy
And peace and death.

—

My ears are called back
To hear the bells of reality
Ringing …! …! …!
Reminding my lungs to inhale.

I exhale all form;
And wait for empty breath
To fill my lungs again
And again
And again.

I exhale all things.

Structures are interchangeable
Chaos moves through everything.

Through every cell.
Through every atom.

Structures are interchangeable
Chaos moves through everything.

Through every thing.
Through every breath.

THE SAVIOR

(38 lines)

I hear the dreams calling out from the archives of memory
I feel the desires of my fears
Pulling words out from my lips with their strings
And their ink — and their blood
And in a - whisper - they ask me:
    What dream do you desire?

This begging of the heart that screams into my wounds:
With beginnings and ends
With beginnings and ends.

Endless satisfaction without breath
Endless pain without death
Endless beginnings with endless ends.

This longing that begs the heart to open
This dream attached to the imagination
This image that wakes up my heart
This memory that excites my will.

I inhale the scent of nature
I release the seed of life
To become one being
The birth of breath
The death of shame
The depth of life.

I hear dreams in the walls — speaking
Memories that tell me to go on and find the sun.

I observe my mask
Naked in my mind

With the warmth
Touching my body

I am in the heat.

I ask the sun
Will you be my friend?
I ask the heart
Will you touch my eyes?
I ask the mouth
Will you kiss me goodnight?

I bring myself through my own passage

Interacting with a particular ritual;
And communicating with an unusual voice.

THE OBSERVER

(37 lines)

There is an eye inside the mind:
An eye that sees itself thinking
An eye that watches dreams
An eye that observes the eye.

I am tired — the conscience
Consciousness — conscious
Yet [...] I am to justify my own existence.

If I am to explore the self
I will be honest and kind.
If I am to seek an unfound sound
I will listen through both ears;
To the sun and to the moon.

If I must move with the wind
I will go into the imagination
And hope to reappear.

If I am my own witness
I will gaze into myself
If I am my own speaker
I will call out with my tongue

And say: Emerge!

Once you are honest
You'll see what prevented you from being honest;
Your future self has already uncovered your future.

There is a witness who remembers the forgotten
And a child who remember her name

There is a prosecutor who remembers
What he intentionally forgot
And ancestors who record
From the end
Back to the start.

And when they arrive
I will tell my story from beginning to end.
When it's time to die
I will have already died
And when it's time to be seen
I will have already seen myself.

For **the eye which sees** — is in — and of — the mind.

THE HEALER

(64 lines)

My head is stuck under a rock I found
In the deep-dark passages of the conflicting mind.

My hands are caught between

A god who holds my fear on his violent spear (and)
A goddess who has pulled my heart apart from mind.

My feet are stuck in the womb of creation
My eyes are stuck behind god's first orgasm
And my soul is on the dinner plates of the elders

Praying: Feed me — feed.
But I am saying: Free me — please free me!

At the peak of the darkest hour:
No hand can hold my heart
No kiss can soothe my tongue
No voice can calm my fears.

Sleep only awakens the screams from the underworld;
Voices that hide behind the - pillow -
Waiting for the night
And my right ear.

Fears wake me
Tears shock me
The sun burns me
The water drowns me

I want to breathe again
Breathe again.

I speak into myself and say:
Breathe into your heart
And I will breathe into your scar
You are worthy in your pain
Your eyes are worthy
Don't be ashamed
To see through yourself.

You don't know what you don't know
You can't know what you'll never know
You know your breath.

Breathe your breath and close your ears to
The war that started before your birth.

Breathe your breath and open your ears to the
Voices that soothed you through your birth.

Allow your panic to melt into the sun!
Although you were born into thought
Although you were born into shame
You are worthy of this pain
You are worthy of your heart
You need not run away.

Your wound is safe
Your fate can wait
You are as you are.

They may never see under your veil
You may never want to reveal yourself.

Let loneliness pass with time
Place a **flower** on your casket
Allow your **tears** to fall into the earth
And mourn **validation**.

You are inside your own ears
Looking through your own eyes
Breathing with your own heart
Through your own lungs.

—

Breathe into your heart a soft color
Paint the world with the sun and the moon.

You may ask yourself: *Why does my heart hurt?*
Why do hearts ever hurt?

Go to sleep without the answer.

Breathe your breath.
You are worthy of breath.

THE TRAVELER

(49 lines)

I walked to the edge of the mind
And looked out past my boundaries;
I found a slave in an empty cave
Who climbed a myth-mountain
That never existed.

I asked the teacher: *Why did you lie?*
 They wanted a boundary
 They asked me to lie!

I walked to the edge of my story
And climbed to the edge of my lies;
I found a fantasy on my necklace
(A montage with pictures and symbols)
And a journey that had no road.

I walked through the minds of the scribes
And opened hidden notebooks;
But nothing was inside.

I asked the mystic: *Why?*
I don't know why — but *who am I!*

Fingers pointing to arrows
Arrows leading to temples
Temples and spaceships
Prayers and misfits.

I walked to the edge of the tunnel
But your directions had an end
And although my visions can deceive me
I have found a poem and a pen.

—
I talk to the edge of reason
And climb up every side
I talk to the rays of madness
Until I fall into a consciousness
That writes words without music
And paints powder with graphite and clay.

I imagine books hidden in vaults
With words that gather devotees
That travel at the **speed of light.**

If light moves in circles
The past is before me
If light leaves forever
I'll never know my future.

But I am to travel
And I am to visit the clowns
And I am to see the rivers
And the oceans
And the flames.

I will walk to the edge of the night
And look into the rising stars
I will talk to the falling planets
And move behind the morning moon
And wake up before the setting of the sun.

THE WARRIOR

(71 lines)

When I walked out of the light
And turned around;
I saw why I had left.

And I heard the voices that told me to leave.

I went to slay the dragon
And expose the demigod;
I found them sleeping in a temple
Of which I did not belong.

I exposed my teeth
To unleash – unleashed

And said:
>   *Who wants to know darkness?*
>   *Who wants to see light?*

What I gave to remove the night
What I did to destroy the fight.

In the shadows
On the dark side
With a hard heart
With a stiff neck
And a heavy mind.

If we are light — they are dark
If we are good — they are bad
If we are right — they are wrong
If our story is stronger than their children
Whose language are we speaking?

The dragon and demigod woke from sleep
And spoke with two voices — saying:
>Come closer — come closer — to see like me
>Fight your own body
>Kill to be free.

And I replied:
>I will never agree
>Not if we cannot see

>That although
>Light reveals and conceals
>And darkness conceals and reveals
>If you hide what you don't want to see
>It won't disappear
>It won't go away.

>*Has darkness arrived to hide*
>*Behind — stories and lies?*
>*Must I abandon the truth*
>*For temporary relief?*
>*Who can see all sides and remain human?*
>*And who can know darkness and remain in sight?*

>When I ran away
>It followed my footsteps;
>When I tried to ignore it
>It haunted my future.

>To be free is to see:
>Good as bad and bad as good
>Bad as bad and good as good
>Right as wrong and wrong as right
>Right as right and wrong as wrong.

And they spoke to me in one voice — saying:

But who wants to be free?
We want the light (but we don't want to see)
We want our eyes (but we don't want to be seen).

Who wants to be free?
To see all visions — we are to be
Both the side of holiness and emptiness:
Questions without answers
Answers without words.

So […] I spoke my last words — saying:
    Light won't remove darkness
    For emptiness can't be moved.
    Perhaps the void is a companion.

—

O darkness I dwell with you
O light I wait with you
O darkness I breathe with you
O light I move with you.

THE CONDUCTOR

(54 lines)

Empty your heart
And put your tongue on this page.

I will tell you everything I know.

Watch me bow
Watch me pray
Watch me dip my hands into this bowl of water
Watch me pour this wax into a mold
Watch me light this flame.

In another lifetime
I would have told you things
Shown you my soul
Explained my fears
Described my mind.

But there are things I cannot say
For speech is formed after thought
And I am still thinking.

The Musician
Scream into the moon
With secret words and hidden sounds
Talk to the mountains
With open hands and closed eyes

Reorganize measurements of light and sound
You don't have to hide.

The tone of my question
Is the depth of my doubt

And the depth of my doubt
Is the peak of my silence
And my silence has nothing to say.

I nurture my heart
And return to my breath.

—

Heart sits between the void
Hands move to hold the heart
I lift it out of my chest
And lower it into my head.
I place it gently
Between two hemispheres.

The legs roll back
The knees fold into the chest
And the head into the knees
Until **I am one**
With myself.

I breathe from within the mind
One large breath
And inhale life.

The center of my being — breath
Worthy of inhalation— breath
Worthy of exhalation — breath
The mind is free to think of — breath
The heart will choose itself.

—

I am the center
Between life and death
Breathe again.

My chest is clear.
Breathe again.

Breathe again.

THE DREAMER

(47 lines)

Through the doorway of the garden
Where the flowers know no time
Over the bridge without a form
I cross the river and disappear
Through the forest of my thoughts
Summer — Spring — Winter — Fall
I cross the threshold — through the door

A child with a red balloon
And a needle.

I ask the child: *Where is your home?*
    I couldn't say — I do not know.

Through the walkway of the garden
Where a friend leads me to see
Beside the bench of my memories
A gravestone that reads: **Remember *Me*.**

Through the maze inside the spider's web
Where the labyrinth hides all puzzles
A willow tree that weeps:
    Why did you leave?

Through the tree house in the garden
A boy and a girl with a happy face
Holding hands
Lonely friends
They say:
    Love — it has no end.

Through the layers of conditioning

Where influence persuades instinct
An executioner who's imprisoned by thought.

I ask her: *Where is your home?*
    I couldn't say — I do not know.

Through the outline of the grass
Where the dragons lick their teeth
Three giants wait for me downstairs.
I ask them: *Is this my home?*
    We do not know
    We are hibernating in the dream world.

Through the gates inside my heart
Where I used to climb the trees
I see a pomegranate
And a full moon
And a shooting star
That reminds me of my first dream.

If I wake up (or fall asleep)
If I never leave (or return);
My dreams have eyelashes
That will guide me when I rise
And catch me when I fall.

(167 lines)

Before creation and destruction conflicted
Before this poem began to change form
Before the second story
Before the first story
Before thought and speech
Before love and ink
Before separation

Before anything realized
Before the mind found beginnings
Before the eyes identified patterns
Before the mouth learned to replicate
Before word.
Fore be. Be.
Before fore.

What was the first story?
Every story has a story:
Stories tell stories.
What was the first story?

Note I
The first story brought fear.
I don't remember the first story
But I heard the sounds
And the story helped me forget.

I was scared
I wasn't running away
I wasn't running away
I just didn't want to remember
I don't want to remember the sounds.

Note II

The first story brought comfort.
I fell asleep inside my ears
Smiling through the night.

Note III

The first story brought laughter.
I don't remember the first story
But I heard the sounds
And the story helped me remember.

> We were happy
> We were playing
> We were splashing.

I remember his eyes
I remember her sounds.

Note IV

I can't forget the first story
But I don't remember it.
I can't see it
But I can taste it.

> Memories remember what they need
> Pleasure moves into pain
> And beginnings reach an end.
> Pain moves into pleasure
> And ends are soon forgotten.

Note V

I remember the first story
I remember forming memory.

Note VI

Memories can hurt the mind

And sting the heart.
Memories cut.
I remember emptiness
It wants to be forgotten
But I remember.

> We don't need safety
> We don't have safety
> We were never safe
> After all — safety is temporary
> And permanence needs no safety.

Note VII

Sometimes I forget everything
Sometimes I remember one thing alone (and)
Sometimes I have nothing to remember.

Note VIII

Stories move
Stories adapt
Safety is temporary
Constancy needs no safety!
It will end when it ends
And begin again — when!

There is a constancy in emptiness
For emptiness is never full
Has nothing to defend
And can never disappear.

Note IX

The first story spoke half the truth.

The second story told a full lie.

The third story was written down.

Note X

I have a first story.
There was a cave
They were whispering
People gathering
They were curious.

I was curious too.

Note XI

Between desire and fear
Between honesty and kindness
Pleasure arrives with suffering
Time arrives with death.

Emptiness has birthed opposites.
Emptiness wears all the masks.

Stories are fluid: Memories are not solid.

Note XII

Something happened.

They had secrets
They told secrets.

Note XIII

I had so much to remember
We loved each other
We didn't want it to end.

Note XIV

You who create webs with thoughts
You who lost yourself inside imagination:
I can see you wondering how far it goes
Questioning if the magic will show you more.

I don't have a story
I don't have a story

You must write your own story.

Note XV
Some stories touch the heart
Some stories move the heart
Some stories hurt the heart
Many stories warm the heart.
But in the end —
All stories betray the heart.

Don't all stories have an end?
Aren't all stories rearranged?

[back to narrative]

Is there a strength that can withhold this change?
Although all stories betray the mind
Tell me a story to warm my blood
Tell me a story I don't already know
Tell me a story I won't forget
Please tell me a story —
Please tell me your first story.

Before words
Before they told stories
I don't remember
I don't remember

I don't remember the first story.

Orphans and stories
Lovers and stories
The story of revenge

The story of kindness
The story of creation
The story of history
The story of ends.
Stories to understand
Stories to reflect
Sentences
Languages
Images
Thoughts
Dreams
Ideas
Words
The meaning
The Book.

Note XVI
Who will remember us?
Who will remember our first story?

Note XVII
We will
We will remember.

I will. I will.

Note XVIII
Language reshapes itself
As it follows its own trail
And births its own meaning
For the future.

Stories are born inside stories
Mystery of mysteries.

[back to narrative]

Above all else
I remember what I remember
And I remember you.

In the end
I will remember
The faces of your heart.

In the end
My eye will view
The inner heights
Of narrative

And I won't have a story to tell

I will just stare
Into your eyes
Forever.

I love you.

THE MATHEMATICIAN

(73 lines)

I plus you
Equals us.
This plus this
Equals that.

Counting — reproducing
Subtracting — dividing
Separating the separation.

The - whole - is one:
Many subjects of one object — existence.
The object has subjects
Many subjects are an object
Many objects become a subject
And each subject is an objection to wholeness.

Opposing forces equals competition
Competition equals war.

Who owns the great ideas?

Us minus us
Equals us and them.
Separation of an object
Creates subjects.

Separation of the whole
Creates parts of the whole
And part of this equals part of that;
A whole that is divided is separated.

This divided

Equals that and that.
This - minus - part of this
Equals separation of this - equals - that.
This times this
Equals this — again.

Many things divided
One object divided
The object has many subjects.

What is absolute?

The end of all numbers is the end of imagination
And the end of imagination is the beginning of numbers.

Perspective is understanding;
    Patterns of order.
Order is sequential repetitions;
    Repetitions of disorder.

Fractions and patterns speak to each other;
The percentage of everything equals one.

Connections and assumptions
Observations and representations
Associations and repetitions
Structures and constructions
Combinations
Moving patterns
Finding patterns
Changing perspectives
Sounds and numbers
Words and spaces

What are numbers?
What am I counting?

Understanding changes form
Numbers disappear in their object
And objects evaporate with time.

What lasts forever?

Numbers and spaces to meet in places
Moments and motions to meet in time
The study of ideas is the rearrangement of thoughts
The movement of words is the language of the future.

We communicate the object
We reason with duality

In fire or water
In hydrogen or oxygen
The skin from the bones
The skull from the flesh
The taste from the will.

Circular measurements — never-ending
Fractals — replicating themselves forever.

Patterns I expected — (and)
Patterns I could-never-have foreseen.

THE GUIDE

(32 lines)

With many heads
I have many minds
With many minds
I have many perspectives
With many perspectives
I have many directions
In many directions

My wings can fly.

To increase the speed and light
I listen to the sounds
To decrease the speed and light
I focus on one tone
To increase the depth of darkness
I defocus from the time

And we're soon released out from the cage
To rise again into the sky.

With many perspectives
I expand my boundaries
In one perspective
I am pulled by its gravity.

There are many ways
And many words
And many moons
And many sounds.

I walk through the threshold
Of undisturbed silence

And it whispers:

> I am waiting.
> *Who told you that you lost your mind?*
> Here I am! Here you are!

So […] now that you know — that we must do it alone
Do it gently.

THE MAGICIAN

(46 lines)

Sentences are word combinations
And words are letter combinations
And letters are sound combinations
And sounds are vibrations
And the vibration of solitude is hidden.

Word - after - word
Association - after - association
Links — Chains — Rings — Loops
Moment - after - moment
From first word until conclusion.

I was taught the sounds
I was taught the letters
Associative sounds to communicate replicated meaning.

I mix the letters in a hat
And pull out words I can't comprehend.
I mix the letters in a bowl
And pull out words I don't like.
I mix the words in a city
And pull out rehearsed sentences.
I mix the words inside the earth
And pull out values I don't recognize.
I shuffle the letters through the universe
And pick a word — and pick a world
Word - after - word
Sound - after - sound...sound...sound.

I am ready for the trick!

Sentences are sounds that have been formed

To influence mind
As a fruit has been formed
To influence taste.

Sentences are sound combinations
Repetitively…repetitively…repetitively
Structured sounds that condition a response
Structured patterns that are the motions of thought
And thought moves body.

Magic is the concealment
Between associations.

The words I choose are already chosen
The sounds I erase are always here.

I select my words from a river
With a rhythm
That restructures meaning.

Behind the curtain — magic is a thought
That has been rearranged in an unfamiliar order;
Letters that reorganize words
Into new sentences.

THE WORSHIPER

(40 lines)

Beeswax on my hands
From a candle I burnt
In memory of the fantasies
That appeared before me
In a sweat lodge
Covered with one thousand blankets
And one hundred thousand threads.

The lava rocks dehydrated my skin
The medicine man frightened me
But I gave in.

I cried and saw the mountains
I mourned and saw the lizards
I laughed and heard the echoes.

Olive oil on my lips
From a lady with seven eyes
And seventy hands;
She anointed me.

Sugar on my back
From a cave I found
When nobody was looking for me.

Salt on my chest
From a jar under a desk
That contained the women who looked back.

Carobs on my ears
From a tree that reminded me
Of questions I could never forget.

Ashes on my chin
From an egg and a cigarette
That reminded me to not forget
About the impermanence of rocks and temples.

I found a ram's horn on my lips
And heard the moans of loss.
I found a rope around my waist
A symbol on my palm
And leather straps around my arm
That stopped the blood flow to my fingers.

I found myself in worship.

I turned around — (and)
Crawled inside — (and)
Changed my position.

(51 lines)

What will be fulfilled — will be fulfilled
What will be unfulfilled — will be unfulfilled
What I move — will be moved
What moves me — will move
What I want — may not want me
What wants me — I may not want.
What I write — will be released
What I think — will be in peace
The thoughts I think — will be thought
The thoughts I never think — naught.

I think what I think
In the tones that I use
I speak from the edge of my view.
I feel what I feel
In the sound of my ear
I move with the edge of the new.

If I am wounded — my blood will flow
If I am worried — my scars will show
If I am silent — my hair will speak
If I am hiding — my walls will see.

When I hide — I am found by solitude
When I seek — my vision turns elusive.

Angel X
You are what you are
You are not what you are not.

Whether I choose what will be
Or whether it chooses me to be

It will be what it will be
And in the end — it will be seen
That it was what it was.

Angel X
The truth hides inside you;
Face it: Stand before your image
Walk into what you always were
And away from what you'll never be.

I react in the way I act
I act in the way I react
I change when I change
I grow when I grow

And fall when I fall.

I speak when I speak
I say what I say
I do what I do.

Angel X
You are what you are

It was what it was
It will be what it will be.

I examine observations
I change my directions
I listen to hear as I seek to know
And speak into this silence.

It sounds as it sounds

I am who I am

It will be what it will be.

THE INVENTOR

(80 lines)

Every tick is precise
Every click locks into predictability.

Clock is reliable — time is not
Rocking pendulum repeats patterns
Motion moves forward
Time measures motion
Changing patterns create the past.

Clock repeats its pattern
Time moves through itself
Time moves towards emptiness;
It counts spaces forever without moving.

A sight that can't reverse
It keeps counting.
It keeps going. It keeps moving.
A thought that never ends
It keeps thinking.

Time is reliable to change.

A measurement between moments;
Moments that don't (actually) separate
Moments that don't (actually) expand
Yet […] the eyes keep seeing what was never seen.

I remember the past — but I am no longer;
My views have changed
My cage has widened
And motion keeps accelerating
As I move away from my origin.

Relative to the absence of all
Existence is motionless.
Relative to the essence of all
Absence is movement.

Outside of all sides;
Inside between sides
Motion and stillness know each other.
Order is measurement:
The past and future are relative to stillness.

In motion: The past appears smaller.
In stillness: The future appears clearer.

I watch the clock and calendar
I watch the sun and compass.

Spaces of blocks
Boundaries in motion
Measurements
Rhythmic spaces pulsing — alive
Organized change — the ebb of the tide
Speed and force and pressure and friction
Pushing and pulling
Turning and clicking
Blinking and breathing
Walking and thinking

Where is the space between moments?

Cycles revolving around the sun
Measurements producing replicas
Of fractions and fractals
Worlds exploding into stars
(How far they seem — how near they are)
Fires in the crust of the earth

And dust storms of the universe welcoming new birth.

There is no movement without force
There is no force without life
There is no life without space
There is no space without time
There is no time without change.

Perhaps movement is appearance
Perhaps I am in the center of stillness;
As a brain dreaming of motion
As an artist dreaming of love
As an eye trying to catch a glimpse of itself.

I go inward and move the earth with my imagination
Until it reflects the colors behind
My motionless deflections.
I look through the light
It looks back at me (with)
Particles of dust
Trying to catch themselves
Before gravity finds the thought
To pull everything — hold everything
Shine on everything.

And it clicks
Ticks — into place
Over and over again.

THE UNDERTAKER

(56 lines)

It is safe to breathe
Your breath.
It is safe to breathe
Your breath is safe.

If they put blindfolds on your eyes
Or chains on your feet
If they take away your teeth
And lower you into the sea

Close your eyes and see.

You are not under
You are not over
The ground is hard
The sky is soft.

Please. Don't worry.

You are inside the air
You are outside the air
In between — air. Air.
We are the air.
Do you feel this air?

Breathe — Breath.

If they take your life
If they remove your safety
If they scare you into fright

Close your ears and hear.

—
Panic and death
Scare.
Sound and silence
Know.
Pain and pleasure
Move.

Please. Don't worry.

—
Go in peace.
Breathe until the end
Where you'll let it go — alone.

In your mind. In your time.

Breath welcomes us into this form
Silence will guide us out.

It's okay to breathe your last breath.
Breathe the breath that's yours
Release the breath that's not.

Breathe your breath
Alone in your heart
With your breath.

And when it goes — go in peace
Let your breath slowly fade
Allow the image in your mind
To slowly drift away

Sailing into peace where emptiness belongs.

Falling asleep
Forever

Please. Don't worry.

Your breath had depth
Your life had breadth
Your breath may rest.

We must breathe our last breath
Alone.